Super Simple Things to Do with Pressure

Fun and Easy Science for Kids

Kelly Doudna

Consulting Editor, Diane Craig, M.A./Reading Specialist

A Division of ABDO

ABDO
Publishing Company

To Adult Helpers

Learning about science is fun and simple to do. There are just a few things to remember to keep kids safe. Some activities in this book recommend adult supervision. Some have objects that pop or stove burners. Be sure to review the activities before starting, and be ready to assist your budding scientist when necessary.

Key Symbols

In this book you will see some symbols. Here is what they mean.

Hot. Get help! You will be working with something hot.

Adult Help. Get help! You will need help from an adult.

Safety Glasses. Put on your safety glasses!

visit us at www.abdopublishing.com

Published by ABDO Publishing Company, a division of ABDO, P.O. Box 398166, Minneapolis, Minnesota 55439. Copyright © 2011 by Abdo Consulting Group, Inc. International copyrights reserved in all countries. No part of this book may be reproduced in any form without written permission from the publisher. Super SandCastle™ is a trademark and logo of ABDO Publishing Company.

Printed in the United States of America, North Mankato, Minnesota
102010
012011

PRINTED ON RECYCLED PAPER

Editor: Liz Salzmann
Content Developer: Nancy Tuminelly
Cover and Interior Design and Production: Oona Gaarder-Juntti, Mighty Media, Inc.
Photo Credits: Kelly Doudna, Shutterstock
The following manufacturers/names appearing in this book are trademarks: Arm & Hammer®, Barq's®, Coca-Cola®, Diet Coke®, Gedney®, Heinz®, Ivory®, Orville Redenbacher's®, Sunkist®, Welches®

Library of Congress Cataloging-in-Publication Data

Doudna, Kelly, 1963-

  Super simple things to do with pressure : fun and easy science for kids / Kelly Doudna.
      p. cm. -- (Super simple science)
   ISBN 978-1-61714-675-6
  1. Pressure--Experiments--Juvenile literature. 2. Force and energy--Experiments--Juvenile literature. 3. Science--Experiments--Juvenile literature. I. Title.
   QC73.4.D68 2011
   531'.1--dc22

                                2010020861

Super SandCastle™ books are created by a team of professional educators, reading specialists, and content developers around five essential components—phonemic awareness, phonics, vocabulary, text comprehension, and fluency—to assist young readers as they develop reading skills and strategies and increase their general knowledge. All books are written, reviewed, and leveled for guided reading, early reading intervention, and Accelerated Reader® programs for use in shared, guided, and independent reading and writing activities to support a balanced approach to literacy instruction.

Contents

Super Simple Science

Want to be a scientist? You can do it. It's super simple! Science is in things all around your house. Science is in a balloon and in a potato. Science is in popcorn and in a soda can. Science is even in water and in soap. Science is everywhere. Try the **activities** in this book. You will find science right at home!

Pressure

Learning about science using pressure is super simple! Science explains why pressure forces a stopper to pop out of a bottle. It explains why a ketchup **packet** bursts when you **stomp** on it. Science even explains why popcorn pops. In this book, you will see how pressure can help you learn about science.

Work Like a Scientist

Scientists have a special way of working. It is a series of steps called the Scientific Method. Follow the steps to work like a scientist.

1. Look at something. Watch it. What do you see?
   What does it do?

2. Think of a question. What is it like? Why is it like that?
   How did it get that way?

3. Try to answer your question.

4. Do a test to find out if you are right. Write down
   what happened.

5. Think about it. Were you right?
   Why or why not?

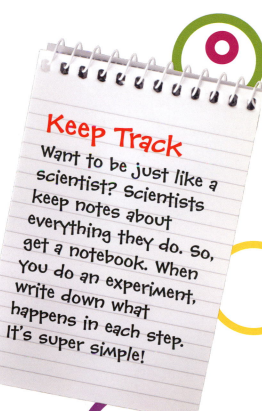

Keep Track
Want to be just like a scientist? Scientists keep notes about everything they do. So, get a notebook. When you do an experiment, write down what happens in each step. It's super simple!

 # Materials

eyedropper

baking potato

drinking straws

2-liter plastic bottle

measuring spoons

ketchup packets

bowl

baking soda

measuring cups

kitchen tongs

bar of Ivory soap

glass bottle

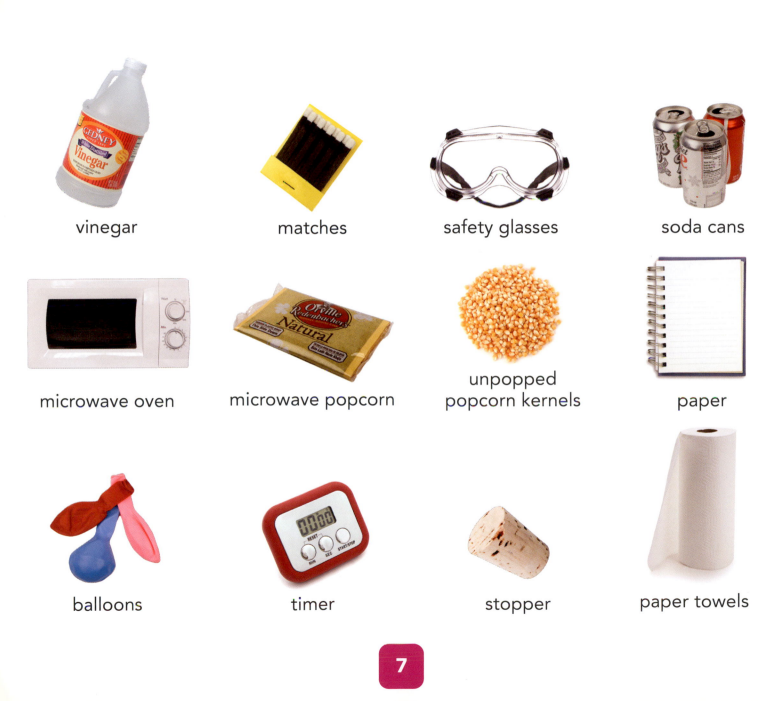

vinegar

matches

safety glasses

soda cans

microwave oven

microwave popcorn

unpopped
popcorn kernels

paper

balloons

timer

stopper

paper towels

Pop the Stopper

What does it take to pop the stopper?

pop

Gas builds up.

What You'll Need
- safety glasses
- empty 2-liter bottle
- stopper that fits the bottle
- vinegar
- measuring cup
- measuring spoon
- baking soda

1. Put on your safety glasses.

2. Pour ½ cup (118 ml) vinegar into the bottle.

3. Put 2 teaspoons (10 ml) of baking soda into the bottle. Hold the bottle away from you. Quickly put the stopper in. Do not use the screw-on cap.

4. Point the top of the bottle away from yourself and anyone else in the room. Shake the bottle. Wait a few seconds. What happens?

5. Rinse the bottle. Do steps 1 through 4 again. Use a little more or less vinegar or baking soda. Does this affect the result? If so, how?

What's Going On?

When you mix vinegar and baking soda, it makes a gas. The gas fills up the bottle. When there is no more room, pressure from the gas pushes the stopper out of the bottle.

9

Drop and Rise Before Your Eyes

Can you make an eyedropper sink and float at will?

The eyedropper goes down.

squeeze

10

Fill the bottle with water all the way to the top.

 Suck a little bit of water into the eyedropper. It should be about half full.

3 Drop the eyedropper into the bottle. The tube should be pointing down. Screw the cap on the bottle.

4 **Squeeze** the bottle as hard as you can. What does the eyedropper do?

What's Going On?

The eyedropper floats because of the air inside it. When you squeeze the bottle, the pressure forces more water into the dropper. This makes the eyedropper sink. When you let go of the bottle, there is less pressure. The eyedropper rises.

11

Don't Mess with Ketchup

Why does a ketchup packet explode when you step on it?

Stomp on it.

12

 **1** Go outside.

 **2** Lay a ketchup **packet** flat on the ground.

3 **Stomp** on it! Aim for one side of the packet. What happens?

4 Use paper towels to clean up. Clean the sidewalk and your shoe!

What's Going On?

Stomping on the packet makes less space inside it. The ketchup can't fit inside anymore. So it bursts through the packet!

13

Potato Plunger

How can an ordinary plastic straw pierce a potato?

What You'll Need
- baking potato (any potato that is longer than it is wide)
- straight drinking straws (not the kind that bends at one end)

The straw goes through it.

14

Hold the potato firmly in one hand. Make sure to hold the potato near the end.

 Pick up a straw with your other hand. **Stab** the potato hard with the straw. What happens?

 Take another straw. This time put your thumb over the top of the straw.

4 Stab the potato again. What happens this time?

What's Going On?

A soft plastic straw is no match for a potato. Putting your thumb over one end traps air in the straw. The air pressure in the straw increases when the straw hits the potato. Air presses against the sides of the straw. That makes the straw stiff. The straw goes right through the potato.

Crush the Can

Can you crush a soda can without stepping on it?

The sides of the can get pushed in.

16

Put on your safety glasses. Fill the bowl halfway with cold water.

 Put 2 tablespoons (30 ml) of water into an empty soda can.

 Set the soda can on a stove **burner**. Have your adult helper turn on the burner.

 Wait until the water in the can bubbles. That means it is boiling. Wait one more minute.

 Hold the tongs with your palm up. Pick up the soda can with the tongs.

 Quickly flip the can over and stick the open end into the water. Hold it there. What happens?

What's Going On?

As the water boils, it turns into water vapor. The vapor pushes air out of the can. When you put the can into cold water, the vapor quickly cools. It turns back into water. That leaves extra room. Air can't fill the space because the can's **opening** is underwater. Pressure from the air outside pushes the sides of the can in.

17

Balloon vs. Bottle

Will a balloon go into a bottle without bursting?

The balloon gets pulled in.

The paper burns.

Part 1: Balloon In

1 Make a water balloon. It should be a little bigger than the mouth of the bottle. Tie it shut.

2 Rub some water around the mouth of the bottle.

3 Have your adult helper do this step. Light a match. Set one strip of paper on fire. Put the burning strip into the bottle.

4 You can do this step. Set the water balloon on top of the bottle. What happens to the fire? What does the balloon do?

What's Going On?

The burning paper made the air inside the bottle warm. Warm air takes up more room than cool air. When you put the balloon on top of the bottle, the fire goes out. The air cools down and takes up less room. That makes more space inside the bottle. The pressure of the air from outside pushes the balloon into the bottle.

19

Part 2: Balloon Out

 1 Rub water around the mouth of the bottle again.

 2 Try pulling the balloon out. Are you able to?

3 Now put a straw in the bottle.

4 Try pulling the balloon out again. What happens this time?

What's Going On?

The first time, the balloon gets caught in the mouth of the bottle. That's because no air can get around it. When you add the straw, it lets air into the bottle. The air pressure inside and outside the bottle stays equal. That lets you pull the balloon out of the bottle.

Microwave Magic

Can a microwave oven help you with science?

The air or water inside gets bigger and the stuff gets puffy.

What You'll Need
- bar of Ivory soap
- paper towels
- microwave oven
- unpopped popcorn kernels
- 1 bag microwave popcorn

21

Part 1: Billowing Soap

1 Unwrap the bar of Ivory soap. Break it in half.

2 Lay a paper towel in the microwave. Put one half of the soap in the center.

3 Set the oven to high. Cook the soap for 90 seconds. Watch it carefully. What happens?

4 Safety first! It is important to let the soap cool for a couple of minutes. Then take it out of the microwave. What does it look like? How does it feel?

What's Going On?

A lot of air is trapped inside Ivory soap. Cooking the soap in the microwave warms and **softens** it. The air trapped inside the soap also gets warm. It starts to get bigger. The pressure of the air causes the soap to form a light and **puffy** shape.

22

Part 2: Popcorn Puzzle

 1 Look closely at a few unpopped popcorn **kernels**. How do they look? How do they feel?

 2 Prepare the microwave popcorn. Follow the directions on the label.

3 Remove the bag of popped corn from the microwave. Point it away from your face. Pull it open.

4 Pour the popcorn into a bowl. Now how does it look and feel? Enjoy a yummy snack!

What's Going On?

A popcorn kernel has a little bit of water in it. Cooking popcorn turns the water inside each kernel into steam. Steam takes up more room than water. The pressure of the steam causes the kernel to explode! That's what makes the **puffy** treat that we love to eat.

23

 Conclusion

Congratulations! You found out that science can be super simple! And, you learned about pressure. Keep your thinking cap on. Where do you see examples of pressure every day?

 Glossary

activity – something you do for fun or to learn about something.

burner – a round, flat part of a stove that gets hot.

congratulations – something you say to someone who has done well or accomplished something.

kernel – a grain or seed of a plant such as corn, wheat, or oats.

opening – a hole that something can pass through.

packet – a small and usually flat package.

puffy – light and soft looking.

squeeze – to press the sides of something together.

stab – to poke something with a sharp object.

stomp – to step on something hard and suddenly.